Poems on Loss, Hope and Healing

Diane H. Schetky

ISBN 978-0-557-07328-3

Poems on Loss, Hope and Healing

"Poetry is, above all, a singing art of natural and magical connection because, though it is born out of one's person's solitude, it has the ability to reach out and touch in a humane and warmly illuminating way the solitude, even the loneliness, of others. That is why, to me, poetry is one of the most vital treasures that humanity possesses; it is a bridge between separated souls."

Brendan Kennelly

Contents

Introduction

As a child, I never liked poetry. In college, I shunned courses in literature for art and requisite pre-med courses. Many years later, while working as a hospice volunteer, I began to use poetry in a bereavement group that I facilitated at Maine State Prison, a maximum-medium security prison located in midcoast Maine. Buck, a member of the Hell's Angels, joined our Healing after Loss group to deal with the death of his father and a failed marriage. His time with us was interrupted by a 30 day stay in solitary confinement for an infraction of prison rules.

Typically, inmates in solitary regress and/or act up. Buck, in contrast, passed his time there writing 80 poems which provided him solace and focus and helped him process his many losses. Upon returning to our group, he shared some of his poems with us. Another inmate asked if he might read them to his wife, noting that Buck's poetry put words to feelings he shared but could never express. He said his wife could not understand what his life in prison was like and that they were having major communication problems. A few weeks later, he reported back to us that his wife was moved by Buck's poetry and that sharing it with her on the phone had given her new insight on prison life and greatly improved their relationship. Some other inmates began writing poetry and I managed to get a few of them published in Hospice newsletters. Inspired by their ability to write poetry, I decided to try my hand at it.

As with the inmates, writing poetry has helped me deal with the losses in my own life that become more frequent as I age. It has also helped me process traumas I've come face to face with or experienced vicariously in the course of my 35 year career as a psychiatrist and as a long time Hospice volunteer. An added benefit has been the joy that comes from sharing my poems and knowing that they have touched or helped someone.

Nature has always been a healing force in my life as is reflected in my poetry. When in tune with nature, one is never alone. Nature bestows daily gifts upon those whose eyes and ears are ready to receive them. In addition, the seasons serve as a constant reminder of the cycle of life in which birth, renewal and death are meant to be.

One comes to admire the survival skills of white tailed deer contending with two feet of snow on the ground in harsh Maine winters. The tiny, five gram, golden-crowned kinglet who winters and thrives here is a model of survival against the odds. Travels to Antarctica and the Arctic have sharpened my focus and sense of perspective and left me in awe of plants, such as the arctic poppy. It adapts to barren tundra and frigid temperatures by keeping company with warm rocks and swiveling its stem to maximize capture of the sun's heat in its cupped petals.

At the other end of the hemisphere, the albatross spends most of his life in flight or gliding on waves. He must contend with inhospitable Antarctic winds and blizzards, going ashore only once every two years to court and raise a family. With a wing span of 11 feet or more, he soars on the prevailing winds thereby getting a boost as he circumnavigates the globe several dozen times during his lifespan of 50-60 years. Nature repeatedly demonstrates that life can trump adversity. We, too, can draw strength from rays of light and learn to soar with the harsh winds that enter our lives.

Diane H. Schetky
Rockport, Maine

Loss

Think of a poem as a little vessel carrying precious cargo,
such as grief, through stormy seas to safer harbors.

Memorial Service

In the soft glow of candles
there is shared grief and hope.
The shadow of my flickering candle
dances around its paper collar.
It is present
but cannot be grasped
or held,
just as it is
with our lost loved ones.

Inspired by a Coastal Family Hospice Volunteers'
annual memorial service

Catheter Prison

He sits alone in the nursing home
next to a bed in terminal decline
in a room too small to ambulate,
and wonders what to do.
The solemn catheter guard stands watch
preferring her TV stories to talk.
His lifeless cane lies at his side,
trapped with him in a prison for those who
pull their catheters out, not once but twice.

He smiles as I enter his room and
try to find space in which to sit.
He tells me about a prostate that got microwaved,
a disease of the mind that starts with A or D,
how sometimes he is not himself and that
he's pulled his catheter out, not once but twice.

He wants to be home with his wife whose
days tick away under the Hospice clock.
He laughs about how their nurse threatened
to pull off his willy wonk if he ever did it again.
"Of course I won't, I've learned my lesson"
he says "But did I tell you, how
I pulled my catheter out, not once but twice?"

Unraveling

Childhood ditties bubble to
the surface in perfect rhyme
while names of grandchildren slumber
 in the recesses of her mind.
"One, two, buckle my shoe"

With generations in disconnect,
my mother looks at me and asks,
"Where was your mother buried?"

Like a stitch dropped from her knitting,
I have fallen from her family tree.
"Two, four, shut the door."

Still Life with Shaving Brush

I open the door of the mirrored
vanity in search of a
nail file.

There stands the doe colored brush
with which my father
lathered his face

and a small wooden bowl
that once held soap.

Heavy nail clippers in a glass
stand at attention as if
expecting his return

but his hardened nails no longer
need clipping and his beard
has ceased to grow.

I hold the brush
against my face and
feel its downy softness.

Beneath the smooth lid of the bowl
that once held soap
a wisp of his scent still lingers.

I carefully return the objects
as if restoring their places in
a Morandi still life.

I have forgotten what I came for
but found my father
in an almost empty wooden bowl.

The Coffee Pot

The white ceramic coffee pot
sits atop the old wood stove
"It's slow," says my aunt "but it
makes awfully good coffee."

I sit impatiently and watch
her morning ritual of pouring in
aliquots of hot water and
warming goat's milk in a pan.

Sensing my need for coffee and
to be on the road ahead of
the impending storm,
she apologizes for the delay.

Icy windows begin to melt.
The sand truck comes and goes.
Chickadees come for a few more
thistle seeds and head for cover.

The slow drip of the pot forestalls
our parting giving me time
in which to admire her focus,
stamina and tenacity.

She hands me a chipped cup
filled with strong café au lait.
It is tepid by now and I wonder
will I do as well at when I am 94?

The Compost Pile

My aunt, Diana, always wanted
to have her ashes scattered
upon the compost pile
in the garden she so loved.

A stubborn Vermonter,
she was not easily swayed.
As death neared, I asked if
she'd considered other options

such as the top of the hill
behind her old farmhouse
where she would be in the good
company of her mother and niece.

I mentioned the splendid view
and peacefulness with only
occasional disturbances
from autumn's hunters.

She laughed at my foolishness,
noting she wouldn't be there to care.
Realizing the decision was mine,
I asked for directions up the hill.

"It is easy, a straight walk up
through the woods to the top.
You will find a stone marker where
we scattered mother many years ago."

The trek was steep and slippery
and the stone now hidden by a
a dense carpet of umber leaves
was nowhere to be found.
At 97, Diana could no longer
be my guide and even the hunters,
who knew the woods better
than I, were stumped.

Following her peaceful death,
friends gather in the yard under
the warm hue of late afternoon light
that softens the November chill.
We take turns scattering Diana's
ashes in our favorite spots and
share memories of helping her weed
beds of asparagus and beans, and

the bear that awoke her from her nap
beneath the shade of the old apple tree
and how she had slowly backed into her
house while keeping one eye on the bear.

The bear continued to feast upon the
newly fallen apples but Diana refused
to be held captive in her home,
especially by a bear.
She grabbed the old hunting horn
that hung on the wall, blasted it once
 and watched the bear retreat.

An elderly friend scatters ashes on
the rose bed near where they sipped
Hu Kwa tea while savoring memories
of travels to their beloved Greece.

I take my turn, dipping the trowel
into the bag of ashes and dust
the crown of eggshells and wilted
weeds on the old compost pile.

I save the last of her ashes for
the raspberry patch and watch
the sun cross over the hill.
The chattering chickadees linger
as the curtain of night descends.

Diana lies dormant amidst the
asparagus, beans, and berries
In the end, she had her way and
we will hear more from her
come spring.

Joys and Sorrows

A father dying of pancreatic
cancer.
A couple announces
their commitment ceremony.

A son killed in combat
in Iraq.
A newborn baby welcomed
to the fold.

A bitter divorce
finally resolved.
An adoptee finds
her mother.

Such are the joys and
sorrows
that knit the fabric
of community.

They long to be
shared, yet
crouch in fear that no one
will be there for them

to listen, to bear
witness,
to share the joy,
to share the pain.

Estrangement

A relationship
transformed that is
no more.
The morning mist
that dissipates.

No cards, casseroles or calls
of condolence.
Silent grief
for what was and
what may never be again.

An empty space
filled with what ifs
and memories.
Hope of reconciliation
precludes closure.

Spitsbergen

Once pristine beach now scattered
with worldly piñatas of Japanese floats,
plastic death traps that once held beer,
ghostly ribs of forgotten vessels and
toys of children who never ventured here.

Such is the garden that closets
above ground graves of explorers
who never made it home.
A nesting arctic skua dives at us and
with anguished cry, she pleads for us
to leave her young and home alone.

White Nights

Through the haze of last night's vodka
I struggle to make sense of my surroundings-
vats of lemons and pickled eggs,
rich brocade wallpaper stained by water,
and a grand chandelier that evokes
better times in St. Petersburg.

This small room in a communal apartment
is home to my friend, Valya, and all that she owns:
an aged sofa, elegant armoire, sewing machine,
handwritten scores of music and
her heirloom sleigh bed in which
she insisted I must sleep.

Strains of shimmering music from *Boris Gudonov*
and Valya's' role of Marina echo in my head.
After our performance, we'd stayed up late
in the white night of a sun that would not set,
drinking vodka while speaking Fruskee,
our private tongue of French, Russian and English.

I asked about her childhood and she spoke
of the Siege of Leningrad as seen
through the eyes of a small frightened child
whose mother kept her by her side
rather than risk sending her to the country
with scores of refugee children.

They made bread from shavings of wood
and ate wallpaper glue to fend off starvation.
The nights were dark, the days were dark,
but oh the cold. Corpses mounted in the streets;
the frozen earth rejected burials.

They huddled indoors for nine months,
venturing out only to scavenge for
food and fuel. They drew their water from
the *Neva* and hoped it would not freeze.
She paused to hold herself tightly,
remembering the cold.

I'd asked what kept her going.
She had replied without hesitation,
with hand upon her heart,
"It was my mother's love,
I could not have survived
in the country without her."

Valya rose early today, tidied
the sofa on which she slept,
wrapped the pot of kashi in newsprint
and tucked it beneath a pillow to stay
warm for me. Before leaving for work,
she left a note reminding me
the bus to the Hermitage is #103.

Checking to make sure I have my key,
I descend the dank stairwell that smells
of urine. The elevator is in disrepair.
Seven flights later, I am on *Nevsky
Prospect* with renewed respect
for the people of St. Petersburg.

A Glacier Crumbles

A mighty glacier recedes
Its massive façade calves,
crashing
into the sea
with a boom
that echoes through the fjord.

Seabirds rush in to
scavenge
ancient sediment churned
by the meltdown.
The milky glacial sea
assumes a muddy cast.

A scrawny polar bear
bears witness as
two cubs frolic at her side.
She scans the waters
for floats of ice upon
which she might hunt.

Who hears the
gasp
of a dying glacier?
Who sees the rivulets of
tears
pouring forth beneath it?

Who feels the
despair
of a mother bear
unable to feed her cubs
in Arctic waters too
warm for ice?

If we cannot feel
their pain
how will we have the courage,
the determination to change
our world
before it is too late?

My Father's Shadow

It has been almost five years
since my father died.
He cast a very long shadow
from which I tried to retreat.

Now, having hatched
from his orbit,
I long to return
to the folds of his shadow.

The dead leave no shadows-
only memories in which
light obscures
the dark.

Cliff Hanger

My icy fingers
grasp
at clumps of tussock grass
above the high cliffs that drop
to the dark
arctic waters
of the Southern Ocean.

My feet falter, I
grope for a foothold on
slick grass while
following the pied piper
of pelagic birders who
leads us to the edge.

I've come this far,
in search of
the light mantled sooty albatross.
His future is threatened by
longliners with miles of hooks
baited with squid.

After 7 years at sea,
he comes ashore to woo a mate.
He's fashioned a nest from
the finest of flora available
on this remote isle that
lies beyond reach of rats.

Word comes that our pelagic piper
has sighted a male.
Through binoculars,
I can see dark eyes and sooty brow.
The young albatross sits proudly
upon his nest that warms the snow.

In response, to a speck above,
he utters his call.
A female swoops from above
with wingspan
of two meters
to inspect his handiwork.

Suddenly, confused by calls
from competing suitors,
she retreats and
performs her alluring aerial ballet,
inviting potential
mates to make their choice.

Once, again, she approaches the cliff
now claimed by our male.
Buffeted by strong winds
she cannot land and
is forced to retreat.

She attempts to repeat
her lithe moves in the sky
but high winds conspire creating
a kaleidoscopic choreography.

The steadfast, adolescent albatross
plaintively calls.
She approaches him, yet again,
with feet flexed ready to alight but
her inexperienced landing gear falters.

She's tossed to the sky where,
exhausted, she rides the winds.
A mere a speck in the blue,
leaving far behind
the faint call of
her woeful
suitor

.

Full Circle

I sit with a man who has raped
his young niece.
He refers to it as an affair
but he's facing 10 years.

I sit with a man rejected by
his family
alone with his shame and
the question why?

I sit with a man who's been raped.
He feels the sting
of stigma and the jeers
of other inmates.

I sit with a man who feels
victimized
by interrogators who suggest
he consented to the act.

I sit with a man in tears
with head in his hands
who asks, "My God is this what I
put her through?"

Aroostook County Unfolding

Dense fog enfolds me as
I head south on US Route One
following on blind faith
the distant lights of a truck
while scanning shoulders
for early morning moose.

By Presque Isle, bathroom and
kitchen lights signal that dawn
is on its way and the harvest beckons.
I begin to make out roadside stands
with pumpkins, new potatoes,
Yukon Gold and a few stray chickens.

Pickups and tractors punctuate the
vast, rolling fields and Full
Gospel churches keep these
families from straying too far.
A sign for Bert's Salvage suggests
that more than souls get saved up here.

The landscape shifts to young pine and
tamarack then Houlton's strip malls as
I turn onto the beginning of Interstate 95.
A color guard of deciduous trees still
muted by fog is my constant companion for
the next two hours on this barren highway.

Flocks of crows hop from road kill
to safety with alacrity and agility
as I disrupt their early morning
routine, the avian equivalent of
morning coffee, donuts and
the latest gossip at Tim Horton's.

The vistas are few and the promised view of
Mt. Katahdin is not to be seen today. I am
left reviewing yesterday's trial in Caribou
and the weight carried by the judge who must
sift through days of testimony and decide the
fate of a man charged with killing his father.

Mud

Soap bubbles blown by a child
bobble across the hood of my car
reminding me of simple pleasures
on this bleak March day.

Trees are blushed with pink
but no sign of green.
A newborn calf lies in the mud,
a promise of what is to come.

A woman and child hasten to
the calf that does not stir.
How to explain to a child so young
mother nature's cruel tricks?

The Glove Compartment

The police search through
looking for clues of
who she was and
how she got there.

An old lottery ticket
with numbers she picked,
a purple schrunchy with a few
red hairs that still cling.

One small bottle of cheap perfume,
an unpaid parking ticket,
thirteen cents in change and a
pack of Menthol Lights.

A greasy napkin from
Dunkin Donuts with
directions to Amy's house
scrawled upon it.

A broken cookie with a
hatched fortune beside it
offering assurance that
"You will soon be famous."

Such is the detritus of
her short life as
she lies dead in her car,
the victim of a homicide.

How She Died

I passed her in a body bag
being carried out the door
and wanted to scream
"Stop that's my sister!"
I had come to comfort
our father who found her.

If not for the rain and
city traffic, I would have
arrived minutes earlier, found
her lying on her bed and
seen the ravages of alcohol
written upon her young body.

Her small apartment smelled
of death and incense.
Our father stood by the window,
numb and at loss for words.
A hug was the best
I could offer him.

Her death was unattended,
possibly intended.
She had led a lifestyle
careless and evasive.
Interventions repeatedly failed
to compete with her first love.

THINK

REUSEFUL

485 MAIN STREET
ROCKLAND, MAINE
04841

207 - 596 - 5600

Useful items created
from recycled material

Alcohol was her default
for dealing with life.
It quenched her thirst,
submerged her sorrows,
dictated her decisions and
distanced her from family.

We will never know what more
we could have said or done.
She took secrets with her,
in keeping with her habit,
leaving family feeling helpless
and with unanswered questions.

She was my only sister,
a much younger half-sister.
A divorce then a continent
kept us far apart.
With her death went any
hope of reconciliation.

We will never know why she died
but only how she died: sadly, alone.

Illness

Illness is the teacher we so disliked who taught us oh so much

Appendectomy

That morning she was not feigning a stomachache
to avoid her teacher who constantly harped,
"Diane is not working to her potential."
She lay still in her warm bed thinking it
would pass if only she did not move. But the pain
kept gnawing at her belly like a hungry beast.

A doctor was summoned who poked and prodded
in places where no one had prodded before.
A blood test confirmed the pain was not of her making
and so to the hospital she was taken
where she was asked to count backwards
while inhaling foul vapors.

As the numbers faded, she ascended
rising higher and higher away from the beast.
As the operating room grew smaller,
she soared lithe as a balloon.
Higher and higher she went, venturing
on her own to places not visited by others.

Back in her bed, freedom was replaced by
doting caregivers and the string of her balloon
by an intravenous line yet, the nascent thrill
of exploration festered and she knew that
she would again break free and continue
her travels to places not visited by others.

Blighted Ovum

I lay in my hospital bed
listening to the cries of
newborn babies and
tears came to my eyes.
A nurse asked if I was afraid
of having a D&C.

I was crying for what was to be
but would never be
not a D&C.
My doctor said it was
a blighted ovum
that was not meant to be.

But who is to say it was
a faulty ovum rather
than an inept sperm?
Colleagues tried to cheer me
with hopes of future
pregnancies,

which offered little solace.
Comfort would come from
a young patient who paused,
while playing in my office,
looked up at me with his
big brown eyes and said

"I bet you are really sad to
 lose your baby."
Many years later, I realize
if not for this loss,
my remarkable second son
would never be.

Captive

I am tethered to a bed
by a catheter and IV.
New sounds assail my head
intruding on my sleep.

There's a machine at my feet
rhythmically pumping my calves
as I twist beneath the sheet,
looking for a spot of comfort.

My infusion pump roars and beeps
providing a low ostenato that
accompanies the PA bleeps.
The head nurse is needed in 204.

A hooting comes from next door
then cries of "help, help, help,"
barnyard bleatings and more.
A soul has lost her bearings.

Bathed in fluorescent light
I shut my eyes and pretend it's
an owl hooting at night.
Sleep is brief; it's time for vitals.

The PA beckons housekeeping
and, once again, the head nurse
then a code blue in 202.
Hospitals are not for sleeping.

Discharge is my best hope
for peace and healing
even if forced to elope.
The quiet of home beckons.

Thyroidectomy

My scar smiles at me
from the mirror each morning
better than a frown

Modern Medicine

Nameless faces
Faceless names
Just the facts
Not the feelings
On to the next patient
My time is precious

Many questions
Abrupt answers
Search the Internet
Read the handouts
Call my nurse
My time is money

Metastases

Mets ascend on high
A shadow on my landscape
Will the sun shine through?

The Slow Train to Healing

This train makes too many stops:
hospitals, labs, radiation,
body scans, dated magazines
and cold, sterile rooms.

This train is too slow.
It brakes when I want to speed,
long waits for test results
and side effects that linger like stale smoke.

This train is remotely controlled.
Where are the conductors and engineers?
Who comforts the passengers
holding the cancer tickets?

This train goes to strange lands.
Women shield their bald heads
 from sun and stares
determination hides their tears

Stop!
I want to get off,
go back to where I was
but
this is a one-way train.
Slow train or no train,
embrace the journey.

I 131 (Radioactive Iodine)

I 131 charges through the
gastro-intestinal highway,
a Sunday outing of Hell's Angels.
roughing up salivary glands
punching out some taste buds
and leaving rubber along the way.

They search for the nearest
thyroid fast food eatery,
finish a gluttonous meal with
satisfying belches then, not yet satiated,
the Angels rumble on
in search of metastatic morsels.

They leave no visible signs of carnage.
Their hostess looks unscathed as
she reposes in bed devouring
a murder mystery while
wiling away her days in quarantine
and sorting out the good guys from the bad.

Inertia

Inertia is a heavy blanket
unwilling to be cast off.
Inertia snuffs out
the flickering
candle
struggling for air.

Inertia, is the fog hovering on the harbor
hiding the horizon.

I must press through it,
find the bells and buoys to guide me beyond
and
rekindle my stamina.
Treks and trips await me.
My patience grows thin.

Beyond radiation

My aura is fading.
Invisible remnants of radiation
dance a polka in my stomach
and boogey in the toilet.
Three flushes later they are warming
the soil above our septic system.

Here a pain there a pain
and any odd symptom
raise the question
is this, could this
be a symptom
of cancer cells that got away?

Today, I went to a lecture
amidst gray haired ladies,
none of whom were pregnant,
so far as I know, and traded
worrisome thoughts for
modern and post-modern painters.

Baking Bread

White caps whipped by wind
race to the shore.
Morning sun begins to wane
and the offshore island,
bundled by snow,
recedes.

A warming oven awaits loaves
of bread. Two friends converse,
double check the recipe,
and wait patiently
for their bread to rise
and wait patiently

for results of a biopsy
to confirm that a cancer
has returned.
The phone rings:
a recorded voice offers
life insurance but no reassurance.

The loaves of bread rise,
are kneaded down, shaped,
gently covered with a damp cloth
and tucked in the warm oven
to escape winter's chill.

The friends dust off their
jeans. Powdery wheat, like
new fallen snow, encircles them.
They wonder if they remembered
to put the iodine free salt
in the bread and wonder

why they became
victims of thyroid cancer?
The bread rises again
and is ready to bake. They
make fine diagonal cuts in the loaves
to maximize the rise

An egg white wash follows,
the loaves go in a hot oven
with a pan of hot water below
to ensure crusty loaves. They wait,
and they commiserate about
the miserable low iodine diet.

They give thanks for the
rhythm of tides and seasons,
a roof overhead and food on
their plates, despite the cold.
For now, they avoid the question of
why and pending radiation.

They dwell
in the moment
enjoying a perfect loaf of
iodine-free French bread,
squash-apple soup
and the bond of friendship.

Written for Katie on her birthday

Nature and Healing

When in tune with nature, you are
never alone.

Healing

To heal is to make whole
or so they say.
Can one ever repair pieces
of a life shattered
like broken heirloom china?

And who can take away
pain that eats away
at the core of one's being
or restore a limb
no longer there?

Pain cries out for a dressing
to cover the wound,
stitches to mend and restore
but healing comes from within
at its own slow pace.

Healing is like a toddler learning
to walk.
His gait is unsteady,
he falls, he bumps his head,
he cries, he gets up again.

Slowly, he gains momentum,
starts to overcome his fear,
explore a new world and
reach for arms that await him.

Slowly, the bereaved find
their way in a changed world
with empty spaces, new rules
and residual pain but

they wonder who
will be there to catch them
when they stumble?

Slowly, they regain their balance
and appreciate what they
have learned on the journey.
Their world holds possibilities
and memories that now comfort.

Cycle of Life

A child holding her first kite
teaches an early lesson of life:
Hold a child too tight and she will not fly
not tight enough and she will be lost.

Grasping leads to suffering
as we cling to the string of life trying
to avoid the pain of loss
while defying the inevitable.

While cluttering our lives
with death defying stuff, we fail
to see the beauty in birth,
the beauty in death and
all that lies between.

One Year Out

The rhododendron leaves curl
like neatly furled sails as
the temperature hovers
around zero.
It is a good day for
hunkering down and thinking.

It has been a year since
my diagnosis.
The cloud of cancer that
followed me everywhere has lifted.
My world has changed
and assumed a sharper focus.

The rising sun is brighter,
the soft sound of rain sweeter.
I surround myself with what
is important,
let go of trivia and
ignore the dust bunnies of life.

I sometimes think my cancer
was meant to be,
to know the fear and worry,
to be there for those
going through the ordeal
to listen and steady their course.

I have learned the meaning
of hope,
the importance of dwelling
on what is possible,
listening to my heart and
making the most of each day.

I no longer dwell in the
scary world of percentiles and
prognoses by stage of cancer.
I am here
to embrace today and
enjoy a new place in life.

Searching in the Woods

Today, I set out to see
what I heard but did not see
yesterday, while
skiing in the woods.

My boots squeak
on newly fallen snow
and poles click
breaking the silence.

I pause to look for
animal tracks but
the snow is too deep
and so I look out

through lichen covered trunks
to mountains of white
tinged with pink
and reaching to the sea.

I turn to glimpse
the sun sliding over the hills
casting shadows on
the shimmering white.

The birds I had hoped to hear
have already taken shelter.
I quicken my stride to stay warm.
and retrace my tracks
through strands of pine

Once back on the road,
I hear knocking
atop a large dead tree
then see a flash of crimson crown,
necklace of white
and a long black body.
hammering away.

Today, I found my
Pileated woodpecker
not deep in the woods
but close to home.

Poplars

Quaking leaves
Little coins of gold
in morning sunlight
hanging on by slender threads
Strength in the face of adversity

Half Moon

Lemon moon lying on its backside
Curled up with thumb in mouth
Cradled by the night

Paddling amidst Icebergs

Paddling through the mist
Crackling sounds all around us
Ice breathing new life

Near LeConte Glacier
Glacier Bay, AK

Lessons from Humpbacks

Majestic cetaceans,
largest of mammals
feeding on tiny krill with
herring for added zest.

Massive ballerinas soaring,
leaping with grace and
synchronizing their moves
in collective bubble feedings.

Musicians composing
new songs each year and
transmitting them across
oceans to distant kin.

Mourners staying close
by their dead
uttering soulful cries
while honoring them.

Might we but learn from
our mighty ancestors
how to eat low on
the food chain.

May we choose cooperation
over competition,
and live our lives with
playfulness and grace.

May we learn to listen
without sonic clutter and
practice compassion for
our earth and one another.

Tundra

Parched polygons, Arctic equivalents
of New England frost heave,
adorn this barren soil.
A trapper's hut, bleached by sun, and
hummocks of peat dispel the myth
of inescapable flatness at this latitude.

A scarlet colored spider plant breaks the white
palette that stretches toward the horizon.
Its roots spread laterally so as
not to tangle with the perma frost.
Stems of pale yellow arctic poppies
gyrate slowly capturing rays of sun.

A courtship of two red-throated loons
on a pond of tundra melt makes me
feel truly blessed, as I watch their ballet.
They mirror each other in perfect synchrony
in a dance that goes on and on until consent.
I applaud with wondrous silence.

Winter Haiku

Fresh snow leaves a map
of happenings during the
quiet of the night.

Deer tracks searching for
rosebuds in winter's first snow.
Disappointment

Angel wings in snow
Talons of a great horned owl
who fed well last night.

Maine Spring

Equinox

Wet snow falls as
the heavens squeeze out
the last of winter.

Rhododendron leaves unfurl
looking for signs of spring then
quickly revert to winter postures.

Frost heaves, lobster boats and mud:
Maine's harbingers of Spring.
Lopsided seasons teach patience.

Turkey Vultures

Two turkey vultures soar
lazily above the pines.
The ripening of winter's carrion
signals Spring's arrival.

Awakening

A red squirrel, emerges from the wall
having survived winter less half a tail.
His nimbleness no doubt saved him
from the clutches of a hungry owl.

A chipmunk, lean from winter's fast,
gorges on sunflower seeds.
The bird feeder with mounting
drifts of snow, is now a drive-in eatery.

Dare devil gray squirrels intoxicated
by Spring, leap from tree to tree.
A male chickadee in search of a mate
trills his new spring song of fee-bee.

A nearby beep, beep, beep sounds alarm.
Not the call of a screech owl but
a bright red bulldozer raping the land.
Another house intrudes upon the forest.

Loon Taking a Bath

The loon, intent upon preening, ignores
my kayak gliding towards her.
She slaps her wings upon the water
dislodging dust and mites.

Gracefully, her neck arches backwards
to ascertain that tail feather are not amiss.
Her head dives beneath her wing
creating a headless apparition.

Then suddenly, like a phoenix,
she rises from the lake,
her splendid white breast reflecting
sky and water.

Her neck shimmies with joy
in celebration of this fine autumn day.
She repeats her ritual several times,
unconcerned by my intrusion on her toilette.

Barbs of feathers are now in place,
oiled and ready to go,
but she lingers on the lake, forestalling
her flight to winter quarters.

Megunticook in the Fall

The loons have departed
along with the summer people.
The lake's parched and aged skin
reveals its bony structures
jutting through the surface
and hints at what lies below.

Empty Adirondack chairs sit
in quiet contemplation as two
young cormorants dry their wings
on ancestral rock adorned with guano.
Rejoicing in the absence of outboards,
I paddle slowly through the maze below.

Maine State Prison

Papillon

An errant Monarch butterfly
alights with grace on a
plum colored coneflower,
in this not quite barren yard.

Indifferent to their crimes,
he gratefully accepts
the fruit of inmates' labors.
A yard is a yard, as long as
you are a butterfly.

As quickly as he alighted, he is gone
having touched persons less
fortunate with hope and
the promise of freedom.

Nocturne

Silently he slithers under
the floodlit fence adorned
with crown of concertina wire
that shimmers in the moonlight.
Unseen by prison guards,
he digs with determination.

An inmate keeps silent watch
through his slit of a window
praying for the safety of his friend,
his only contact with the world
that lies beyond the wire.

He feels the pangs of loss and
envy, watching him waddle off
with belly full of grubs as he
squeezes under the fence from
whence he came, his dorsal white
stripe shinning in the moonlight.

Touched by an Elephant Seal

It is a grizzly, gray day
in King Haakon Bay.
Icicles drip from tall tussock grasses
that rim the snowy peaks of remote
South Georgia Island in the Southern Ocean,
and icy rain pelts our faces.

We are here retracing the steps
of Ernest Shackleton,
who landed on this beach with
five of his men after 16 days at sea
traveling 800 miles in a open 23 foot boat
in weather far more wretched than this.

I should move about to stay warm
but choose to sit quietly,
huddled in my hooded red arctic jacket
observing "weaner" Elephant seals
barking and playing in a tidal pool.

At 200 lbs they are on their own as
their mothers have taken to sea to refuel.
I sit at a respectful distance, mindful
of the dictum "Don't do anything
to alter their behavior."

A curious seal pup lumbers out
of the pool and towards me,
showing no fear of humans, whom
he's never met before.

He nuzzles my shiny, black Wellington
then starts to press harder on my boot.
Unable to find any mother's milk,
he starts to explore my upper body.
Mindful of not altering his behavior,
I look to our guide for direction.

The pup's curiosity turns to her
and he crawls upon her lap,
gives her a wet smack on the cheek
then waddles back to his playmates.
Surely, Shackleton never received
such a warm welcome here.

After the Storm

The battering nor'easter
has moved up the coast.
The plowmen rest
in deep but brief sleep
after a night in whirling
white up to two feet deep.

The droning of plows
has abated for now.
The village turned white
by the wintery night
awakens to the sounds
of snow shovels scraping.

White pines sagging from
snow and ice entwine
reaching out to touch
one another other
for reassurance that
they still stand upright.

Utility men arrive
from neighboring states to
rectify nature's wrath.
Offers of hot coffee
and snowshoes abound to
help the men scale the mounds.

Severed limbs of white pine
lie limp upon the snow.
Early spring-cleaning has made
way for new growth below.
Wounds of these ancient trees
will heal, as in years past.

Neighbors open their homes
to those without power
with offers of a warm shower.
Hardened old timers stay at home
keeping watch on their pipes
and roofs laden with snow.

The Internet, schools and
shops will sleep in today.
TV deprived children will
play the old fashioned way.
People will reach out and
and touch one another today.

The Gift

It can't be purchased in
a store or online.
It never goes on sale.
It is precious yet affordable
but remains a scarce
commodity.

It comes with two ears
but no set of directions.
It is easily overridden by
life's distractions but,
when used regularly,
bears fruit.

The gift of listening is
a gift that goes on giving
It says "I hear you" and
"I am here for you."
It does not pass judgment
only care.

Acknowledgments

I wish to thank the many people who have offered me encourage-
ment and advice regarding this book, including Hilary Carr,
Kirsty Karkow and Kathy Deupree, all dedicated hospice volunteers, and my partner, David Wiggin. My sons, James and Scott
Browning helped with editing. I also wish to thank the many
inmates who have participated in the Healing after Loss Group
for giving me inspiration. In addition, they affirm man's capacity
to deal with adversity and have demonstrated that, all too often,
anger masks pain and that empathy begins to flow once in touch
with one's pain.
        Part of the proceeds from the sale of this book will go to
Coastal Family Hospice Volunteers of Midcoast Maine.

Painting on front cover by Kathy Deupree
Brendan Kennelly quotation from www.thewritersalmanac.com,
April 17, 2009

Photo on back cover of Diane Schetky by Tim Arruda

Previously published poems

American Journal of Psychiatry and Law, Vol. 34, no. 1, 2006: Aroostook County Unfolding, The Glove Compartment, Papillon, Nocturne

American Academy of Child and Adolescent Psychiatry Newsletter: Jan/Feb, 2005: Unraveling

Off the Coast, May 2007: Still Life with Shaving Brush

The Puckerbrush Review Vol 26 (2), 2009: The Slow Train to Healing, I 131, Beyond Radiation

The Aurorean, Fall/Winter 2006-2007: Megunticook in the Fall, Winter Haiku

About the author

Diane H. Schetky is a graduate of Sarah Lawrence College and Case Western Reserve University School of Medicine. Prior to her retirement two years ago, she practiced child, adolescent, adult and forensic psychiatry. For the past ten years, she has run a bereavement group at Maine State Prison for which she received the Governor's Public Service award for volunteerism in the public sector. She has written and/or edited five books on child forensic psychiatry, one of which received the Guttmacher Award for outstanding contribution to forensic psychiatry. This is her first book of poetry. Diane is a long time resident of Rockport, Maine.